KEEPING WATER CLEAN

by Courtney Farrell

CHERRY LAKE PUBLISHING • ANN ARBOR, MICHIGAN

Published in the United States of America
by Cherry Lake Publishing
Ann Arbor, Michigan
www.cherrylakepublishing.com

Printed in the United States of America
Corporate Graphics Inc
January 2010
CLSP06

Consultants: Jeff Clark, associate professor of geology, Lawrence University;
Gail Saunders-Smith, associate professor of literacy, Beeghly College of Education,
Youngstown State University

Editorial direction: Book design and illustration:
Amy Van Zee   Emily Love

Photo credits: Stanislav Spurny/Shutterstock Images, cover, 1; Shutterstock Images, 5,
7, 17, 22; Dorling Kindersley, 9; Gerri Hernández/iStockphoto, 11; Claudio Zaccherini/
Shutterstock Images, 12; Jill Fromer/iStockphoto, 15; Al Braunworth/iStockphoto, 19;
iStockphoto, 21, 27; Karol Kozlowski/Shutterstock Images, 25

Library of Congress Cataloging-in-Publication Data
Farrell, Courtney.
  Save the planet : keeping water clean / by Courtney Farrell.
     p. cm. — (Language arts explorer)
  Includes index.
  ISBN 978-1-60279-659-1 (hardback) — ISBN 978-1-60279-668-3 (pbk.)
  1. Water--Pollution--Juvenile literature. I. Title. II. Series.

  TD422.F37 2010
  363.739'4—dc22

                              2009038095

**Cherry Lake Publishing would like to acknowledge the work of The Partnership for 21st
Century Skills. Please visit www.21centuryskills.org for more information.**

TABLE OF CONTENTS

You are being given a mission. The facts in What You Know will help you accomplish it. Remember What You Know while you are reading the story. The story will help you answer the questions at the end of the book. Have fun on this adventure!

Your mission is to learn about Earth's water. Earth has a lot of water. But clean water is so scarce that many people do not get enough of it. If there is so much water, how can usable water be scarce? How does water get polluted? What can we do to prevent water pollution? How can you help conserve water so everyone gets enough? Follow our field team as they travel around the world learning about water. Be sure to remember What You Know during your mission.

WHAT YOU KNOW

★ Earth's surface is about 70 percent water. Most of this water is in oceans.

★ Most of Earth's water is salty, such as ocean water. Only a very small amount is freshwater that we can drink.

★ Earth has always had the same amount of water throughout its existence. The water changes form. This is what drives the water cycle. Water rains down from clouds. Then, it evaporates and goes back up into the sky. The water never runs out.

Most of Earth's water is in the oceans.

★ Polluted water has dangerous chemicals or bacteria in it, which can make people and animals sick.

We are going on a field trip around the world to see how people use water. Join us on this exciting adventure!

First, we visited Spain, a country in Western Europe. Some places in Spain get very warm in the summer. People from all over the country go to the beach. We visited some children who were playing with a garden hose outside their beach house. They were having fun! But soon, their mother told them to turn off the hose. They were wasting water and raising the family's water bill. In Spain, as in the United States, most people have to pay for the water they use. It isn't free unless you have your own well. Wells are deep holes that have been dug in the ground. If a well is dug in the right spot, it will fill with groundwater. Then the groundwater can be pumped to the surface.

A World of Water

The children wanted to know why they could not use all the water they liked. After all, the ocean is full of water. At their beach house, the ocean was right outside! And they wondered why they couldn't water the lawns with ocean water. Ocean water can't be used to water plants because it is too salty. Salt water makes plants wilt. If lots

Playing in the sprinkler is a fun way to cool off in the summer, but it can waste a lot of water.

DESALINATION MAKES SEAWATER INTO FRESHWATER

More than 97 percent of Earth's water is in the oceans. The salt can be removed from ocean water in a process called desalination. This process is expensive. Many desalination plants have been built in Spain. They have also been built in the Middle East, a region rich in oil.

of salty water gets on land, that land will never be good for growing plants again. People can't drink salt water either. Consuming salt makes people thirsty. Thirsty people who drink salt water get sick and feel even thirstier.

After the children turned off the hose, the driveway began to dry out. Where did the water go? It evaporated, which means it changed from a liquid to a vapor. Water vapor is light and rises into the air. Once it is high in the sky, the vapor joins together to form rain, snow, or hail. The water is heavy and falls back to Earth. Water goes around and around in the water cycle. The world has the same amount of water now as it has ever had. The water you drink today might once have been slurped by a cave man! ★

Water evaporates and goes into the atmosphere.
Then it falls down to Earth again as precipitation.

On our way around the world, our field team stopped in Africa. We visited a remote village in a country called Malawi. Malawi is in southeast Africa. Here in this village, women walk miles each day to get water for their families. Most houses do not have plumbing. People can't turn on a faucet to get water.

We met a woman who was leaving the village to get water. We walked with her. She carried a big jug. It would hold approximately 5 gallons (19 l) of water. This would weigh roughly 40 pounds (18 kg)! It was a long walk on a hot, dusty path, and we were tired. When we got to the water, we were surprised. The villagers collect water from

WELLS PROVIDE CLEAN WATER FOR AFRICAN VILLAGES

Volunteers often dig wells in developing countries such as Malawi. Rain soaks into the ground and collects there. The ground filters this rainwater. Wells allow villagers access to clean water. Clean water helps people stay healthy. Many people donate money to dig these wells.

AFRICA

Malawi

In many places in Africa, villagers walk long distances to get water.

a pond. The woman poured the pond water through her shirt. This filtered it, but it still looked murky. This water is what her family uses to drink and bathe. There is no other source of water for them.

While we were there, we saw animals drinking from the pond. Their droppings make the water dirty. The dirty water contains germs that sometimes make the villagers sick. We learned that many people in the world do not have clean water. ★

Our field team arrived next in the Jiangsu Province of China. Jiangsu is on China's east coast. It has many beautiful rivers and wetlands. Some cities have so much water that canals run between the houses. Some people here travel by boat.

Throughout China, the water is in trouble. Most of the rivers and lakes are polluted. The water is not safe for drinking. Some water is polluted with human waste and chemicals. The sewage makes the rivers smell bad,

Some places in China have a lot of water, but it is not always safe to drink.

SEWAGE TREATMENT PLANTS

Human waste has germs in it, so water polluted by sewage can make people sick. Sewage treatment plants can prevent this. These plants clean the wastewater that goes down toilets. Once wastewater is cleaned, it can safely go back into rivers.

and it kills fish. We walked along a river and saw dead fish floating in the water. Many people live in China. The country is very crowded. The cities do not have enough sewage treatment plants for all of their people. The Chinese government is working to build more sewage treatment plants to clean up the water.

Pollution Problems

The Chinese government has passed laws against polluting water. The laws are not always followed, though. People who pollute are not usually punished. In China, factories often dump toxic chemicals into rivers. Toxic chemicals poison people, plants, and animals.

In 2008, China hosted the Olympic Games. The world noticed China's pollution problem. People were concerned about the health of the athletes who might be exposed to the pollution. The Chinese government wanted to make a good impression. Chinese officials worked hard to clean up pollution. ★

Back in the United States, we investigated water conservation in the desert state of Arizona. Most people in Arizona save as much water as they can. Today we visited a house with a beautiful garden. The garden was watered with rainwater only. It doesn't rain very often in Arizona. This house had a rainwater catchment system. Its purpose is to catch and save rain. Rainwater that ran from the roof into a rain barrel was used to water the garden. The garden was full of drought-tolerant plants. Drought-tolerant plants do not need much water to survive.

Water-Saving Habits

At this house, special pipes catch and recycle gray water. Gray water is water that was used in sinks and showers, but not toilets. It can be reused to water the yard. Plants can still grow if the water has a little soap in it.

Inside the house we learned more water-saving tips. They were easy! Flushing a regular toilet uses 3 to 7 gallons (11 to 26 l) of water. This home had an ultralow flush toilet that used only 1.5 gallons (6 l) of water per flush.

Some plants can thrive in places where there is little water.

We learned to shut off the water while we brush our teeth. This saves lots of water. It is also good to take shorter showers. We even save water while doing the dishes. We used to run water while we rinsed dishes. Then we loaded them in the dishwasher. Not anymore! Now we put some water in the sink and rinse all the dishes in the same water.

We felt good about our new water-saving habits. You can save water at your house, too. ★

USING WATER IN THE GARDEN

Gardens and lawns need water to grow. There are many smart ways that gardeners can keep their gardens green and conserve water. It is best to water in the morning or in the evening. When the air is cool, less water evaporates off the soil. Also, it is best to water plants slowly until they are thoroughly drenched. This means the water goes deep underground. The plants can then soak up water from below in case of a drought.

There are many ways to save water around the house.

Next, we visited a ranch in Wyoming. Here, we saw cattle raised for meat. Raising cattle uses a lot of water. On a hot summer day, a steer will drink as much as 18 gallons (68 l) of water! The grass that cattle eat also needs water to grow. Because it doesn't rain much in Wyoming, the grass needs to be irrigated. Irrigation means watering crops with water brought in through canals or pipes. The ranchers showed us how they use irrigation to water the grass the cattle eat.

Irrigation has been used for thousands of years. Some places are so dry that it would be impossible to farm or

HOW MUCH WATER DOES A COW USE?

It is hard to know exactly how much water it takes to produce meat for the market. One estimate is that it takes 12,009 gallons (45,460 l) of water to produce only one pound (0.5 kg) of beef! This amount includes water the steer drank over its entire lifetime. Those gallons also include water used to grow all the food the steer ever ate. Beef cattle have short lives. It takes only two years for them to grow big enough to send to the market.

Irrigation systems help farmers water their crops!

ranch without irrigation. Many places in the United States and around the world experience droughts. Droughts are long periods of time when there is no rain. With irrigation, farmers don't have to rely on the weather to keep their plants watered and healthy. Irrigation makes farming possible during these long dry spells.

Some ranches are near rivers. These ranches use river water for irrigation. Most places in Wyoming are far from bodies of water, so people there use well water. ★

July 25:
PESTICIDES IN IOWA

We have moved on to Iowa, a Midwestern state. Here, farmland stretches for miles around. We visited a farm that grows corn. The farmer explained to us that all this farming can cause water quality problems. He said that in the Midwest, there is usually enough rain for farms. The problem here is that many lakes, streams, and wells have become polluted with toxic chemicals used on some farms.

Insects, Weeds, and Water

Many of these toxic chemicals are pesticides. Pesticides are poisons that people spray on crops to kill pests such as bugs or weeds. Pesky insects can do a lot of damage to crops. Bugs will eat holes in fruits and vegetables. Then nobody wants to buy them!

Herbicides are special pesticides made to kill weeds. Weeds compete for space with crop plants. They also reduce the amount of crops produced. Weeds grow quickly and choke out the good plants that farmers are trying to grow. Insecticides are made to kill insects that are harmful to crops. However, insecticides also kill helpful insects such as honeybees and butterflies.

Some farmers spray pesticides on their crops to keep bugs away.

How do pesticides get into our water supply? People spray pesticides in yards and fields. Then the chemicals wash off when it rains. These chemicals flow into gutters, ditches, and storm sewers. From there they go into wetlands and rivers. They poison the animals and plants there. Pesticides have been found in 90 percent of water and fish samples taken by the U.S. Geological Survey. Frogs often have deformed offspring when they live in pesticide-contaminated water. Some of these deformed frogs have missing or extra legs.

Chemicals that run into sewers can pollute water supplies.

These chemicals can also contaminate wells that people drink from. Contaminated water contains pesticides in such small amounts that people are not able to taste them. This water looks clear and tastes fine. Pesticides are poisonous to people, too. But it usually takes a lot of exposure to pesticides for a human to become very sick.

Communities with contaminated water have higher rates of cancer. This disease can be deadly. Pesticides are especially dangerous to the workers who spray them. These workers can breathe in pesticide mist or spill chemicals on their skin. They get cancer much more often than people who are not exposed to pesticides.

You can help by asking your parents not to use pesticides around the house and yard. Buying organic food also helps. Food grown without toxic chemicals is better for us. ★

ORGANIC FARMING

Organic farmers grow crops without using toxic pesticides. They control bugs in other ways. Some keep chickens or ducks because these birds eat bugs. Organic farms also grow plants that attract helpful insects such as wasps. Wasps love to sip nectar from flowers, but they also eat insect pests.

Our field team's last stop was in beautiful upstate New York. The forest here is cool and shady in the summer. The forest is beautiful, but some of the trees are damaged. They are leafless, especially near their tops. Some are even dying. This damage was caused by acid rain.

Polluted Rain Hurts Forests

Acid rain happens when smoke from factories mixes with water in the air. The mixture forms acid that comes back down to Earth in rain and snow. This acid harms plants and fish. Because of the water cycle, pollution is carried from the land to the atmosphere and back again. Smog from cities travels all around the world this way. Acid rain can come down far from where the pollution was formed. The acid rain problem is worst in the northeast

HOW YOU CAN REDUCE POLLUTION

You can help reduce pollution! Encourage your parents to walk or ride bikes instead of taking the car. If your family is thinking about buying a new car, suggest a small one that gets good gas mileage. This means the car will be able to drive farther using less gas.

Acid rain can kill many trees.

part of the United States. Some lakes that once had fish and frogs in them no longer do.

One way you can help reduce acid rain is by using less electricity. What does electricity have to do with acid rain? Power plants make electricity by burning coal and oil. When people use more electricity, power plants burn more fuel. This causes more air pollution. This air pollution goes up in the air as smoke, but it comes back to Earth as acid rain. This is how air pollution leads to water pollution.

Controlling air pollution can help the acid rain problem. Earth's air and water are connected through the water cycle. If we stop polluting the air, the water will be cleaner. There are simple ways you can help. One way is to shut off lights when you're not using them. ★

MISSION ACCOMPLISHED!

Great job! You have learned many things about Earth's water. You've discovered that water can be scarce on this watery planet, because seawater is too salty for people and plants to use. You have learned how to protect our water by avoiding pesticides and creating less pollution. You have found out many new ways to conserve water at home. Congratulations on a mission well done. Now we're all inspired to save water in our homes and gardens!

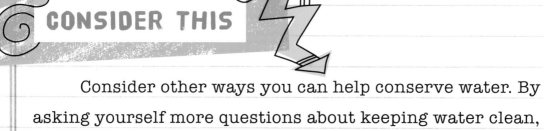

CONSIDER THIS

Consider other ways you can help conserve water. By asking yourself more questions about keeping water clean, you might just start a mission of your own!

★ What can you do to reduce your exposure to pesticides in water?

★ How can you reduce the amount of electricity you use?

★ How can you help conserve water so that everyone gets enough?

★ What are some other ways we can prevent water pollution?

Water is a precious resource.

GLOSSARY

acid rain (ASS-id RAYN) rain made harmful by air
  pollution

atmosphere (AT-muss-fihr) the air that surrounds Earth

bacteria (bac-TIHR-ee-uh) tiny living things that can
  be seen only with a microscope

conserve (kuhn-SURV) to use something carefully to keep
  it from being lost or wasted

contaminated (kuhn-TAM-uh-nay-tid) polluted with
  bacteria or traces of poisons

desalination (dee-sal-ih-NAY-shuhn) the process of
  removing salt from water

evaporate (i-VAP-uh-rate) to change from a liquid into a
  vapor that rises into the air

gray water (GRAY WAW-ter) water that was used in sinks
  and showers but not toilets

groundwater (GROUND-waw-ter) water within the earth
  that can be collected and used for drinking water

pesticide (PESS-tuh-side) chemical used to kill insects,
  plants, or animals considered to be pests

pollution (puh-LOO-shuhn) harmful substances released
  into the air, soil, or water

scarce (SKAIRSS) in short supply

sewage (SOO-ij) waste that is often carried off by drains

toxic (TOK-sik) harmful to the health of people and the environment

water cycle (WAW-ter SYE-kuhl) the ongoing process by which water changes form and moves between land and the atmosphere

LEARN MORE

BOOKS

Strauss, Rochelle. *One Well: The Story of Water on Earth.* Toronto, ON: Kids Can Press, 2007.

Vanderwood, Jill Ammon. *What's It Like Living Green? Kids Teaching Kids, by the Way They Live.* Charleston, SC: BookSurge, 2009.

WEB SITES

The EPA's Environmental Kids Club

http://www.epa.gov/kids/water.htm

Research water conservation and other environmental issues.

U.S. Geological Survey's Water Science for Schools

http://ga.water.usgs.gov/edu/index.html

Find out about the water cycle, keeping water clean, and many other topics.

FURTHER MISSIONS

HOW TO SAVE WATER FOR YOUR GARDEN

Rain barrels are a great way to save rainwater for later use. Just put a rain barrel outside your house under a downspout. When it rains, the barrel will fill with water. You can use that water in the yard. Rain barrels are easy to buy online or in stores. Just remember two things. First, put a lid or screen on it. This keeps mosquitoes from breeding inside. Second, don't drink the water unless it is filtered first. Learn more at http://www.epa.gov/Region3/p2/what-is-rainbarrel.pdf. Have fun!

BE A WATER CONSERVER

Many Americans use water every day to bathe, brush their teeth, do the dishes, wash clothes, and water their lawns. This water usage can really add up! But you can reduce how much water you use. Don't run the water when you brush your teeth. Take short showers. Also, wait to do laundry or run the dishwasher until you have a full load. Being careful of how much water you use can help preserve the precious resource. Encourage your family and friends to do the same!

ABOUT THE AUTHOR

Courtney Farrell taught biology and microbiology for ten years at Front Range Community College in Colorado but is now a full-time science writer. She has a master's degree in zoology and is interested in conservation and sustainability issues. She lives with her husband and sons on a ranch in Colorado.

ABOUT THE CONSULTANTS

Jeff Clark is an associate professor of geology at Lawrence University where he serves as chair of the environmental studies program. He received his doctorate from the Johns Hopkins University, and he has undergraduate degrees in geology and environmental studies from Middlebury College.

Gail Saunders-Smith is a former classroom teacher and Reading Recovery teacher leader. Currently she teaches literacy courses at Youngstown State University in Ohio. Gail is the author of many books for children and three professional books for teachers.